Marketing Basics You Have to Know

Do you want the learn the fundamentals of marketing, but don't want to spend a lot of time? Then you've come to the right place! In this short book, we will talk about the most prominent concepts in marketing. Marketing skills are highly demanded in today's world, in almost any industry sector. This book offers you a short and concise overview of the most prominent concepts in marketing. No long and boring lectures, only the necessities, presented in an accessible and visualized way with multiple real-life examples! My intent is to teach the fundamentals and inspire you to dive more in-depth in the fascinating discipline of marketing! Moreover, I thrive to provide the best value possible at an accessible price point for literally everyone!

This book contains :

❖ **Section 1: To begin with...**

- *Definition of Marketing & why marketing matters*
- *Basic marketing terms*
- *Market segmentation*

❖ **Section 2: Marketing mix**

- *4P's marketing mix*
- *Products*
- *Pricing strategies Place*
- *Promotion*

❖ **Section 3: Relationships with customers**

- *Bonus lecture: Consumer Psychology*
- *Personal selling tips and tricks*
- *Building relationships with customers*
-

❖ **Section 4: Planning & Forecasting**

- *Marketing plan*
- *Bonus lecture: SMART goals*
- *Forecasting*

❖ **Section 5: Marketing Research**

- *External environment*
- *SWOT Analysis*
- *Bonus lecture: Ansoff matrix*
- *Collecting Marketing Intelligence*

❖ **Section 6: Branding & PR**

- *Branding*
- *Brand positioning*
- *PR activities*

❖ **Section 7: Marketing budget**
- *Marketing budget*

❖ **Section 8: Bonus lecture & Last words**

- *Ethical Issues in Marketing*
- *Last words for this book*

About this book :

How's and why's behind marketing made easy

Section 1: To begin with...

Definition of Marketing & why

I want to talk about the definition of marketing and why marketing matters as a study marketing was first introduced in the U.S. in 1950s all people single marketing sales. I will explain what is popular believe is far from the truth. American Marketing Association defines marketing as follows. Marketing is the activity set of institutions and processes for creating communicating delivering and exchange offering that haveli for customers clients partners and society at large are I it merely a transaction between two parties buyer and seller marketing. On the other hand you have all the systematic planning and realization of business activities to identify and fulfill customer needs. In other words marketing is not about sales. It's about making sales possible. Marketing campaign isn't focused on the short term exchange or sales but a long term relationship building which is beneficial to both parties. Now you know what marketing really is. You might ask why does it even matter. First successful marketing build demand for products and services which in turn create jobs by contributing to the bottom line successful marketing. Also those firms to more fully engage in socially responsible activities. Second Matsu managers median salary in the US is one hundred thirty thousand dollars in 2016. Also the U.S. Bureau of Labor Statistics report that employment of Marta managers expected to rise faster *than the national average for all occupations from 2014 to 2024. Marty Manger is also a role that can work in almost any industry sector surd the success of multiple organizations and individuals is largely contributed by exceptional marketing campaigns. Take Coca-Cola Nike or even Barack Obama's presidential campaign as good examples as we can conclude the marketing manager is a great career choice. Being college demanded highly paid and flexible. Furthermore with months in practice are beneficial to individuals firms and society as a whole. We know the importance of marketing.*

Basic marketing terms

We're going to examine the core marketing concepts. Namely markets needs and demands. First of all kind of marks are out there. We can distinguish Forty-Eight capital markets consumer markets those are mass consumer goods like cosmetics or beverages business markets those are business to business transactions consisting of well informed professional buyers. Global markets same as consumer markets but on a global scale nonprofit and governmental markets those are nonprofit organizations with a limited purchasing power like churches schools and charitable organizations. Well there are several markets are operating in the most important use of monitors is dissatisfied because you emotionally is Maslow the human hierarchy of needs. They may serve as a guideline for money managers to target their market and pay the specific type of needs first of their fees are logical. It's like water food shelter and clothing those type of needs are satisfied by food production firms and the real estate firms. Secondly safety needs those are security health and property. This type of needs are satisfied by insurance companies for instance certain social needs friendship family sense of connection. So step of needs are satisfied by baseball clubs that stores force self-esteem needs. Those needs are self-esteem confidence and achievement. Companies that seek to satisfy this type of needs are BMW tippling and Nike. You may *question why Nike BMW cars and shoes are basically shoes and you're absolutely right. However BMW or Nike strive to make their offering exceed beyond its physical value. DMW are BREMAN cars that can bring your self-esteem to social status up like you present the shoes of successful people like Michael Jordan. Like it isn't used as regular issues but as an issue. Last but not least there are so virtualization needs means having once full potential. Morality creativity problem solving skills making those of needs are satisfied by Harvard University and Gadgil church for example. Now we know what their needs are human beings have a firm should present an offering that can successfully fulfill this needs. It is worth noting that our needs and wants are backed by the ability to pay which is the definition of a demand. There are eight stages of demand. First negative demand. One consumer is like the product. Second non-existent demand. Consumers may be unaware or uninterested in the product Surt lot and demand consumers share a strong need that cannot be satisfied by an existing product force declining demand. Consumers begin to buy the product less often Fyffe the reglued demand consumer purchases on the seasonal monthly or weekly basis since food demand consumers are educated person the product seben overfull demand more consumers would like to buy the products that can be satisfied. And last on holsom demand consumers may be attracted to products that have undesirable social consequences like alcohol and cigarettes. In each case marketers must identify the underlying causes of the demand state and Thurmont a plan of action to shift demand to more desired state. Now you're familiar with basic Marketing concept. Some talk about market segmentation.*

Market segmentation

We're going to talk about market segmentation market segmentation is a process of defining in subdividing large markets into clearly identifiable segments having similar needs and demand curve to just make your segmentation aspect are geographic. Those aspects include nation state regions etc. demographic characteristics like age family size gender income occupation and so on. So replicate terrorist acts such as lifestyle values and personal traits. And last but not least behavioral characteristics those are needs and benefits and also price sensitivity market segmentation is the process of finding a perfect customer for example perfect customer for Tesla Motors would be a millennial with relatively high income growth concern for the environment in evaluating market segments. You must look at two factors segment overall attractiveness and the resources and objectives. Big businesses like Coca-Cola may go for mass marketing. Basically to serve all customer groups with a single offering. Another example frequently observable is in the cosmetics industry is differentiated marketing when the terms so different products are members of different market segments. If however those options are not possible we can go for a single segment specialization. When you target only one specific niche. For example products only target people with very high income want to manifest *their social status market segmentation is an important step in the Volta marketing research. When you try to target a specific group. Follow these guidelines. Population sample should be accessible neatened the population are specific and differentiate the population samples should be measurable. All right that's the simple.*

Section 2: Marketing mix

4P's marketing mix

Now you were densify do customer profile. It's time to market your offerings. What clever marketing researcher named Joe McCarthy proposed a conceptual framework called for a piece of marketing or marketing mix. The main reason this concept is still widely used today is that it simplifies marketing strategy in two main key aspects. Those for using good product or what you sell price . In other words how much do you charge place where do you sell promotion. How do you reach customers. I've chosen BMW to present how marketing mix works in the field was that straight into it product. Both of BMW is high luxury automobiles. Price is a premium pricing throughout the place. Global sales have more than one hundred and forty countries promotion. The use aggressive advertising on TV billboards magazines and online in the lectures . We're going to talk about the variables of marketing mix more and apps. Stay tuned.

Products

We're going to talk about product. The product is a starting point of the overall marketing campaign products combine physical attributes such as color shape and design with psychological benefits such as value and quality. Jurgen zation develops its own brother system which is a group of different products that are related to each other and can function together in order to stand out from the competition. Porter has identified three main strategies that can be used by an organization to have the competitive advantage over the others. First because leadership is the strategy in both reaching high market share by appealing to cost conscious consumers. Basically your costs as much as possible and provide the least expensive option for a consumer. Companies that succeed is using this strategy are Daskal right near an IKEA. Second differentiation strategy. It means making one personal attributes of your product unique to set apart from the competition. Think about the design of Apple iPhone. When it was first introduced in 2007 or recently emerged Amazon stores search focus strategy you adopt a narrow focus and choose a very specific market niche where but competition is rather weak Sinko for all x in the production of watches and Rolls-Royce cars. Which strategy to apply depends on your product offering budget and your desired outcome. These *examples might help you to get a hint of how you should approach positioning of your own product in the market.*

Pricing strategies

We're going to talk about pricing strategies basically price them on the money. The consumer must pay to receive the offering and is the only element of money to mix with generates revenues. There are several pricing strategies which we're going to discuss right now premium pricing. Price are so hard and those of competitors premium pricing is used to communicate the level of quality you can think of Starbucks and disregard market penetration pricing. Prices are lower than those of competitors to draw attention away from them after the words of the brand has increased from start to increased prices of Chinese for manufacturers like say only psychology. Pricing is a technique which marketers use to stimulate purchasing decision on an emotional level. That's why we see Linus Sansone a price tag not one dollar economy pricing. Prices are set low to attract the widest audience possible. Examples include Wal-Mart and Aldi price giving because a pricing strategy in which marketer sets the relative the initial price for the product or service. First down or the price over time last forever .Those promotional price includes a discounted price or a limited time offer that we usually see in stores last discriminatory pricing. Company sells the same product at several prices depending on the location of pipes. You pay 50 cents in grocery store one dollar in a vending machine and $2 in the cafes.

Place

We're going to talk about the place in terms of place but I have two options for business physical stores and virtual tours. We're going to examine that Ventures a feature of them the advantages of virtual stores include lower prices because there are no physical facilities required. Also time efficiency. Online shopping is faster flexibilty you don't even need to leave the house to make a purchase. Documentation in a sense that you'll probably always know what you're looking for and almost unlimited choice has been on Amazon and eBay. However Aventuras a physical source include physical evidence. You can actually touch the product before you buy it. It's more personal. You can get advice from a real person in case of uncertainty. Last but not least leisure think of shopping centers and IKEA stores. People come there just to have a good time. The choice between visual and physical force is crucial for your business. If you're just starting out e-commerce store is no brainer since it's cheaper and easier. However if you want to move on and expand your business you will need to add physical facilities as well.

Promotion

We're going to talk about promotion as was previously mentioned promotions or means by which you acquire customers is greater we could purchase it goes without saying the core aspect of promotion is advertising. we're going to English several types of advertising with specific examples. Afterwards we're going to talk about ways that you can find your customer without further ado. Let's get started. There are four main types of advertising. First and foremost if advertising it is used to create brand awareness second persuasive advertising it does to influence the customer in favor of a bursting specific product or service. Surd reminder advertising in front speaks for itself. It is used to remind your target audience if your product or services to make them repeat their purchases last reinforcement advertising it convinces buyers that they made the right choice. All these types of advertising are useful depending on the current state your business and your Brummer ago. Now let's talk about where you should put the ads. You can pull your ad some TV radio Internet or in print form. Each of these has pros and cons which we're going discuss right now. TV ads are we are demonstrating broad attributes and portraying user imagery. However it's expensive and target customer may overlook the message print ads print ads have little private information and they're not expensive. However there study by nature and have a short shelf life. Radio ads are really flexible inexpensive but they like visuals and there a less chance that you'll reach your desired purchaser if the letters are relatively inexpensive. There are more advanced targeting options and it's easier to measure the effectiveness of your advertising campaign. However you should consider advertising overload of people nowadays just block consumer tools and they will never even see your advertisements. There are also too many choices and too much competition. It's hard to keep up on the Internet where to put you as the bad mostly on your budget and knish. If you're watching your photography business career or publishing as in journals on the other hand if you're immersed in a new band specific radio broadcasts might be a way to go. If you've already established a strong business then TVs are top big although the most expensive one Internet ad so far are the most flexible easy to make and cost effective you can pay to publish your ads and high traffic websites like Facebook or YouTube or Google or other search engines to appear on the top of the page. The Internet can be used regardless of the size of your business. Being a top choice as your first pick as you acquire more customers. Consider other source of fats but don't be overwhelmed by all that. Singles are they have zero advertising policy yet they have a successful business.

Section 3: Relationships with customers

Bonus lecture: Consumer Psychology

We're going to discuss some interesting insights on consumer psychology. A marketer is a psychologist in some sense. So understanding the psychological processes in the customer's mind is definitely important. Before we dive into the customer decision making process is so fundamental and discussed how human perception works. Hobos have a different world outlook and different opinions on various things. All due to sweep perceptual processes first selective attention. This means that we're more likely to notice a signal from the environment if it relates to our current need. We've all been sure that if we're going on the street and you see a billboard with delicious looking food the promote a certain restaurant. Obviously if you've just eaten you would notice billboard but if you're really hungry then this billboard believe it impose in your mind there is a much bigger chance that you actually go the restaurant and order something. Second process is selective distortion. It is a human tendency to interpret information in a way that fits our own perception. That's for all of our expectations and biases come from. For example I live in the Netherlands. Dutch people generally want the best value for money. There is no such thing as social status. It's perfectly fine for a wealthy person to go grocery shopping in regular stores and it is taken for granted. But what about traditional Chinese who say that's a different story. Their social status is a very important thing for both impersonal buy cheap products. It will hurt his reputation so that process is the selective retention. His visits were more likely to remember benefits of products that we own and forget benefits of competing products. A great example is up. Apple has a massive fan base and those fans believe in Apple so much that they don't consider that other companies might offer a better product even for a cheaper price. That's how successful Apple Marsi campaign has been over the years. All right. We have a hint about human perception. We just got the five stage model of buying decision process. So what are these five stages. First problem recognition. This is the first step in any purchase. Customer identifies a certain problem or need in service for a product that might offer him a solution. Information search in this stage customer doing his research may look for online reviews with probably descriptions or opinions of his friends or evaluation of alternatives. Customers comparing the product that got him interested with other similar products look for the best value with his current budget force purchase decision foggily customer makes a purchase. There are certain rules of some which customer pays his final decision. I'll leave all scientific terms and I will explain using simple language. First of all Kazuma set a minimum to benefit and look for a first option that pops up. The problem though is yourself sometimes when you buy something simple like a shampoo. Normally you don't spend a lot of time compress tons of different Shampoo's write your minimum subtable shampoo might be the one that is not expensive and the suitable pro-male. Once you found the Shampoo's it does the job. No work you no longer consider other options. Secondly because you may choose a brand specific important attribute for example if you buy a car and your most important concern is safety you might get a car from Volvo. Safety is the main benefit of those cars. That's of some is elimination by aspect in this model cause and eliminate different options one by one comparing different aspects. For example if you're buying a new smartphone you might approach it like that. OK. All these smartphones have great screens but this one has a camera so I won't buy it. And then you compare different aspects in the same manner when all available smartphones and you only find the one that suits all of your needs. Ostap is post-purchase behavior. If customers are satisfied or dissatisfied he will likely share his opinion either. But don't kid friends or writing an online review for instance.

Personal selling tips and tricks

We're going to talk about personal sewing tips and techniques. It is important though especially when you're just turning out and don't have any employees or colleagues at this table so might maybe even your only option. Basically person something occurs when you meet face to face with a customer. Think of card use and disregard or Bursal sound grew worse all the time. You won't be able to reach an extremely broad audience. However it has some advantages namely it's more personal. You can customize your own proposition to every individual customer. Also since you're giving each customer a lot of attention and you use your bosal trace is therefore easier to make a powerful impact on a person and make a sale. There is a number of steps involved in personal selling which are prospecting searching for customers and choosing the ones that are most likely to pay for your product or service. Remember time is your most valuable resource. Do your research and don't waste time on customers who are less likely to purchase you are offering. Second. First contact. You have to make the first step. The customer can buy product from another seller in no time. It's up to you to contact your customer whatever it is digital message letter or phone call to reach your customer and start building a relationship. Third presentation trouble call benefits of your service. Be positive about what you're doing but don't push too hard it may cause an undesirable consequence of customers thinking that you tried to deceive him or for overcoming objections. No matter how good your service is there will always be objections. Sales people developed a wonderful method called Spin technique which might seem to stand objections and presenting your Afrique as situational questions. Those questions are to determine the current situation of your client desires and budget and so on. Let's take an example. Let's say you're a wedding photographer. You may start by asking Have you ever been on the show before. How many guests will be at your wedding. But do not ask how much money are you willing to spend. People may not know that themselves used in the right questions. If a couple is having a wedding in a small restaurant you can figure out that they are on a budget yourself. Same goes for the opposite scenario. The problem questions each customer has a problem. Otherwise they wouldn't be talking to you. Ask what you experience last time or for a shoot. Ever been to another wedding before. How do you feel about picture that came out on this wedding. Maybe a friend of a bride paid by your father first and results were of no exceptional quality and the price isnt even aware that she is making the same mistake. By implication questions when you phoned customer problems trigger them make them sound like a big deal. Persuade your customer that if they go to the last charging photographer they will miss out on quality and end up dissatisfied and make it stand out even if the problem is not that significant. You can make the customer feel like it is. But be careful. Find the focus point stay was that there are no products or services that are perfect and can solve all problems. So figure out what you are doing better than others. The state was coming back to the wedding photography example. Potential problems might be the cost of your services. Make them feel that your services are worth the price and if they hesitate to Belfast an amateur their Beecher's will make them happy.

Make it sound like a big deal. Don't say that you will do the best job in the world for a low price. This is simply not possible. If your price is a premium make clients feel that it's worth spending an extra penny and you pay off questions. This is for the value of your service or product comes in. Human beings naturally want to get the best quality for the lowest price but there are always tradeoffs. If you invested all of time and money in your business as top gear many years of fuel experience and so on your service can be cheap. And clients understand that there are many tradeoffs. The most common one is my spend and always receive. Show your client that your service is a solution to their problem. They were looking for. This technique can help you influence the customer to make a purchase. Fifth step personal suck. Close a deal. The customer is ready. Make a call to action and create a sense of urgency. Examples may be the price is limited only for X period. Good luck with your opportunity. This additional benefit or a discomfort is a one time offer my services and don't miss that. It's her last follow up. Stay in touch with your customer. Make sure that everything goes smoothly and you're always ready to assist them in small things such as birthday cards remind clients that you care about them they they're more likely to repeat purchase and spread the word about you those tips and tricks for help in any industry you're operating in. Use them and your skills will grow dramatically.

Building relationships with customers

We're going to examine some tips and how to build good relationships with customers they companies face their toughest competition ever. Consumers are about to switch between brands with one click of a mouse. Therefore long term a mutually beneficial connection with your customers should always be at the top of your priority list. Let's begin with a fairly simple question What does every customer want. The government will say they want to maximize their perceived value. Basically customer perceived value is the difference between the benefits the customer is getting or total customer benefit which they are offering. And the cost has to make or sole customer cost to make it simple. Let's look at it as a formula customer perceived value equals customer benefit minus total customer cost just quite total customer benefit and total customer cost in a bit more detail for customer benefit versus the perceived monther value of economic psychological and functional benefits that the customer gets. So customer costs were first of all the cost customer has to make the price but also time and energy spent on evaluating adopting the product as well as psychological costs such as lots of other alternatives. Every time you buy the product this cost benefit analysis is in your head although you never notice that because it comes naturally. Lets say I want to go to my friends to play pool and drink couple of beers. I have recently heard about the new popular place in the city center. However it will take a lot of time to drive there and it's also quite expensive there. Not mentioning that the place is always crowded so I'll have to wait for a while until were served. Although this new pope has a good reputation I just won't go there because costs exceed my benefits. Come to that place would be too troublesome. On a couple of beers and play ball. It's just a real life example of how it works. All right that's what customers want. But what the way marketers want to maximize the customer lifetime value is more or less the same thing but taking from our viewpoint one to maximize our profits which is our main benefit. At the lowest cost possible. The reason is so-called customer profitability analysis. We try to estimate the maximum profit you're going to make per serving each individual customer or trading customers is always more expensive than reminding them of yourself. You can serve everyone is free to direct their efforts in converting regular customers into customers because customers are more profitable. The person running your product or service on the wants is better not to expect too much. This person can focus on those that buy some frequently because your budget and time are not infinite. But you might ask why is it unusual or beneficial for Argo's to maximize the value for customers. Which in turn maximize profitability for us. That's a win scenario. There are a variety *of ways to make and retain world customers such as customer empowerment. When customers call on the product. Share ideas and demonstrate their passion. That's what the Commerce and the widows did. Also frequency programs are designed to reward customers who by frequently think of stamps in grocery stores. Last but not least membership or VIP programs they open more possibilities to customers that are interested in regular purchases. A good example is Amazon Prime.*

Section 4: Planning & Forecasting

Marketing plan

I want to start by saying that any marketing strategy won't work if you don't have a plan. We're going to talk about what the goal multiplier should look like marketing plan is a written document or a blueprint that outlines key aspects of your strategy based on a specific period of time. Usually it's one year good marketing plan should include your current situation analysis where you are now in the market what's your market share. So who is your target market. We discuss market segmentation in the previous lectures. Some of your broad goals what you seek to achieve in the future. These are methods and controls but we should seek to attain the desired outcome. What tools are you going to use. How are you going to reach customers. Financial projections estimated cost of your marketing Roger. And here's a tip. Venture to estimate your profit. Focus on three possible outcomes. Most like the one pessimistic in case something went wrong and optimistic if something goes better than expected worst. Your unique selling proposition What are your so and how your service can be distinguished from those of competitors having a much simpler serve as a guideline for you and your colleagues to focus your efforts on clearly defined objectives. Take the resource section. Include a link for a website. You can find example of a good marketing plan. Be sure to check it out.

Bonus lecture: Smart goals

We'll discuss how those had smart goals. Now I'm going to give you a very simple framework which is widely used among managers who can use it not only marketing but in your daily life as well. Smart stands for Specific Measurable action oriented realistic and time base. Those are the characteristics of smart goals. Now let's give you an example. My goal is to become rich as soon as possible. You probably guessed it was Margo. In fact it's a dumb goal. It's not specific which is a vague term. 100 bucks is a lot of money for someone. And for another person that might be nothing. Secondly this example being rich can be measured again. Being rich won't be able to people next year really action oriented. There is no action both in this go billions of dollars surely won't pull your head. So this goal doesn't have any plan of action then the goal is not realistic. What are the chances of becoming rich over night. Very small chance. Therefore it's unreliable to pray for doubt. Last but not least this is not time base. As soon as possible doesn't mean anything. Five years may sound like real soon for me and it might feel like a long time for you. So we've reviewed the Dombo. Now we make it smart shall we. My goal is to earn passive income by investing $1000 in the stock market I have a return on investment of 10 percent at the end of the year. Let's apply our criteria again is Pacific. Yes I know exactly what I'm going to do to you my goal is measurable.

Absolutely not Zetlin how much you want to invest and how much you want to profit in the end. Now it's achievable. Sure why not. If you know how the stock market works that's certainly possible. Is true stick now. There is always uncertainty involved and unfortunately not all of your goals will come true. Going to investment in the stock market over a year seems quite unrealistic. If you're not an exceptional investor like Warren Buffett by generating a 10 percent return is not a dream it's perfectly attainable for most people. Lastly this goes time based on Also getting that passive income will take a year. So I have clear expectations. I want to mention that I don't necessarily recommend investing in the stock market that was just an example to get a clearer picture of smart goals. I suggest you remember this framework and use it when you set goals for yourself or your marketing campaign.

Forecasting

We'll talk about forecasting. First of all this forecasting media marketing forecasting is basically anticipating what will happen in the future under a certain set of conditions in Haiti. U.S. companies invest a lot of money in the oil industry because they expected oil price to rise rapidly. But in reality all these Shakespeareans a huge down turn. This is an example of a bad forecast. It is needless to say that market for ecasts is an essential element of my research. But what we actually want to forecast first of all will start with the total market demand total market demand is expected demand for products will be bought by the front customer group in a specific market. There are several steps in all forecasting that all market demand. First defining the market was the size of the market was the target audience. We should take a look at Suppes two products are all completely different. Like Mac and PC or are they hardly different from each other like sold the emotional baggage that sold in stores but are unlikely to distinguish them by any means except the price. Second stop as the main driver of demand. You should look at it from a macro and micro perspective macro level the big picture for example. You are the world for a society Greiss and soulless purchasing power. People are likely to spend money on products that they couldn't afford before. Like cars or jewelry for example micro level means something that is specific to industry. Let's look at a camera industry. Now these cameras are expected to go reduce and forget resolution has all this record and that a b are not in demand anymore. That's why camera manufacturers like Canon filter that quickly experience a *decrease in profits so it's that sense still channels is the main question is what conditions dramatically changed the demand. For example customers love to have a good quality camera on their smartphone but they don't really care about technical specs as long as the picture looks good. Simple consumer doesn't care how many megapixels Apple has. We see that manufacturers are competing for certain features such as portrait mode or slow motion recording but not for a number of megapixels because the megapixels not a driver of the most bizarre features are nice single woman for cars. Is the industry grows. It is basically how the whole industry is developing. For example some companies operate in a highly competitive sector and they always come up with bright ideas to find new customers. But now think about the backbone industry. There's not a lot of room to develop. The focus is to retain customers in the shadows. Mother of high importance company is to operate. She said not to develop such as tobacco or oil industries are now trying to diversify their production to meet new customer demands. Last but not least we had a sales forecast which is basically dead but the volume of sales in a given time period. Usually marketers use the market buildup now and that means identifying all the potential buyers in the market and estimating their purchases as a starting point. You can multiply the expected number of buyers but every quantity each of them purchases times the price as we discussed makes reproductions. Optimistic pessimistic a realistic dissuade can be better prepared in case for rapid change. All right. Now that we know what winter forecast is some it is because the methods by which we're going to do it first muleteers market test market does a kind of experiment a company launches a new product in a limited market to get more insides of how likable your product is there is sufficient demand complete and an official launch of the product to cover up the whole market. One benefit of this technique is that it minimizes the risk and case for uncertainty. However there is a drawback that competitors will observe your offering and either take actions such as copying your ideas or taking price cuts to make leave the market Cytomel its correlations. Now we're talking about statistical analysis basically want to estimate our sales based on the other variables. We're interested in the drivers of demand. Think about touchscreen phones 10 years ago they were a major driver of demand on certain smartphones but noticing that everybody uses there's simply no demand on phones with old fashioned buttons. A benefit of this technique is well it's predictable and easily measurable. A drawback is this kind of analysis can only be reliable in stable markets. If the market is changing dynamically like consumer electronics this form of analysis may be completely unreliable. So the coach is expert opinion. Now this technique is really straightforward. You've asked experts in your field about their expectations of the future the smell might be useful since you're getting more insight from knowledgeable people in this sense. This technique has a high quality drawback is obvious predictions are often inaccurate and may be unreliable. Think of the example about oil companies in the beginning. Experts aren't necessarily right.*

Section 5: Marketing Research

External environment

We're going to talk about the external environment. It goes without saying the business doesn't exist in a vacuum. On the contrary it is shaped by the environment. If you want to be successful into analyzing the Parmentier operating in and come up with solutions to that customer needs first of all need to be aware of fats trans mega trans fats or short list products that are unpredictable by nature. They're very popular at first but quickly fade away. Examples include a yoyo and spinner trans are quite predictable and relatively long lasting. They can provide you pretty good direction for business in the long run. For example messengers are overtaking social networks and stream content is overtaking downloadable content. Those are current trends. Megatrend is a large social economic or psychological change that is forming for years and impacts a major part of society like clean energy robotics industry globalization virtual reality etc.. This way I respond to fast trends magazines. You must be able to identify and analyze major forces of the external environment. Those forces include demographic economic social cultural natural logical and political legal. This analysis is important. If your business is internationally oriented Let's describe this for us and give you some examples. First demographic forces they include population age population growth and fertility rate. For example Netherlands and Germany experienced population aging because fertility rate is quite low. But life expectancy is very high. Second economic forces that represent the condition of countries economy sick of us. In 2008 during the recession consumers were worried about their basic needs rather than self-esteem Heaslip jewelry. It also includes income distribution. Think of strong middle class in Western Europe versus huge gap between poor and rich people in Russia and India. Certain social cultural forces de-code cultural beliefs traditions and consumer psychology for example showing semi-naked women is OK in the Western world but not in the Arabic countries for natural forces represent environmental regulations. They're very strict and Finland quite strict in the US and not strict at all in China or Nigeria. Fix that you got forces that represent all that logically advanced and innovative a country is Japan U.S. and South Korea are among the best in this regard. Lost political forces that influence business legislation for example and in turn protect companies from unfair competition. They also include politics and rights of interest groups such as Greenpeace movement.

SWOT Analysis

the analysis is a matter to work Waldman's strengths weaknesses opportunities and strengths strengths. What is the source of your competitive advantage. What do you do better than the others weaknesses. What holds you back what could improve opportunities. What do you plan to do what you want to do this or are you interested in what makes your competitors vulnerable stress. What problems are there in your industry. What obstacles can stop you from moving forward. What are the goals. It's just a handy framework which can be used for multiple purposes not just marketing research. It's a very simple concept and you've got a hint of what's what. Now this is all about. Applied to the gay side of HP. HP strengths include strong brand wide range of products good reputation and publicity and high market share weaknesses or we should build our presence in certain markets like tablets degrees in revenues in recent years and many cases of inconvenience customer service opportunities for his bill would be to step into new markets like 3D printers or the are to invest more in research and development to present more need based offerings and to focus on other developed markets such foolish being slowly dying market sectors like DC that are still dominant in each piece business and also secure competition in place of Astor's Apple lack of a doubt and so on. That analysis was of course not the most *difficult one. But now we have an idea and you can easily apply to any other business.*

Bonus lecture: Ansoff matrix

We're going to talk about a popular model among marketers called once of matrix. It was developed by eager up in the 20th century but it's still relevant today. The Matrix itself shows for strategies to grow your business and risks that are associated with each of them. Let's talk about each strategy more in detail. Market penetration is simply expanding sales of existing products. This is the most risk free approach in the Matrix but it also doesn't offer a lot of opportunities. Pro-development means introducing new products into your existing market. This market is already riskier but can be more rewarding as well. Market Development refers to putting an existing product into an entirely new market. Think of Coby's you. It's absolutely the same as regular Coke. But there is no sugar Coca-Cola didn't make a new product. Rather they changed the existing product to appeal to different customer group such as people on a diet. This option is even riskier but beneficial in the long term diversification. Bouvard discuss this strategy in a different context. Let me remind you the versification stands for introducing new products into new markets. We call it innovating. That's what Moscow is trying to do with Space-X company. This strategy is the riskiest one. There is a lot of uncertainty involved but this has the highest potential. Your innovative idea can become a real cash cow like iPhone was for Apple and the Matrix is a very simple framework that will *help it. The Durman which direction your business should take and what kind of risk is involved.*

Collecting Marketing Intelligence

Data collection is one of the key activities in marketing research and a big part of marketers job. Bear with me. It's easier than it sounds. Basically marketing intelligence refers to relevant information regarding organizations markets. That is a day to review new market opportunities and assist in decision making. There are multiple ways to get her money in intelligence. We're going to discuss them right now. Internet. The easiest way to collect the available information you need. Basically do your own web research look for independent customer reviews ratings and expert opinions. Amazon YouTube. Quora public blogs Facebook. Just name a few can help you to get a broad overview of what your customers think about your product or service. The Internet can also be used to collect intelligence on your competitors. Keep in touch with sales people. They're the ones that have the most valuable information you need. Ask them to do research from a financial perspective and report their findings accurately. Develop close relationships with urbanisation when you're working with says their profit for a large part depend on yours and vice versa. You've got to keep warm and tight relationships. If you do that will certainly help you to get more information regarding their field of expertise. That might be a G-6 for example with your *complaints response to everything complete on time and do your best to fix the problem. You can purchase Turser information from specialized agencies or firms such as Bloomberg online service questionnaires and focus groups were just stumbled upon them in previous lectures. Very convenient and straightforward way to get information. The last use digital technology is to your advantage. For example hoping to track down the history of every use of your web site. You can also review how much time the average user spends. We're reviewing this particular web page. This way you can identify certain patterns and habits of your audience. All right guys. That was a brief introduction to collecting. MARTIN There are reasons.*

Section 6: Branding & PR

Branding

We're going to talk about branding American Marketing Association defines the brand as a name term. These aren't simple or any other feature that identifies one sounds good or service as distinct from those of other sellers having a strong brand gives you a major edge in a competitive market. It also allows you to easily introduce new products and enhanced credibility. Let's take a look at top five brands of 2017. Those are Apple Google Microsoft Coca-Cola and Amazon. Now Apple has the most valuable brand in the world. That is estimated to cost around one hundred billion dollars. If you want to have a thriving business some brand is a must. The brand is simple The first thing that makes a difference in your products from others and communicates the level of quality to customers think of their expectations when you see an iPhone and Neubrunn phone for instance. The question you might be asking what actually makes a good brand. Well key characteristics of successful brands are audience knowledge. The unique proposition consistency memorability brand interests like your declaration of the heart and soul of the brand which are generally short phrases like seem different or just do it. They're successful because they memorable last year promise. Marketing experts developed a brand name experiment and the strength of the brand. You might also think of it as Karaka brands. I will explain the churchly presence to I know about it. Relevance does offer me something. Performance can a deliberate advantage offer me something better than the others and Boulding nothing else beats it. All the successful brands mentioned previously can reach the top of the brand pyramid which is bottom level value of your brand is build upon three aspects. Knowledge preference of consumers and financial situation to gain insight into how knowledgeable and likeable your brand is . You will use both quality and quantity methods. For instance please pass an Amazon design question use to get an overall view of general perception about their services. Alternatively if you want to go more in-depth you can bring focus groups to understand the underlying problems or things that could be improved in terms of financial analysis. Look at your revenues market share which is the percentage of overall sales in your industry and growth rate which has potential to expand your business as profits increase. Right now to know what mainstream brands prefer to find out whether the brand is strong. Let's talk about branding strategies that firms use. First brand extension using an established brand for a new product. Think of Starbucks ice and grocery stores second Sobran combining your brand with an existing brand single feedback's FedEx Express FedEx Trade Networks etc. or better brand existing brand that gives birth to an extension or Sabran. Think of Coca-Cola of Coke Light zero carb diet that. Well the Baron brand is already associated with many products. It becomes the Mostert brand such as Coca-Cola *dimple or I guess now we know everything that you need and perhaps even more about branding.*

Brand positioning

We'll talk about brand positioning. First of all what's positioned in this case positioning is that of designing and offering to occupy a specific place in the minds of consumers. Successful brand positioning leads to clear customer expectations an important concern concerned brand positioning is looking at and analyzing competitive brands the with the so-called competitive frame of reference to the context in which consumers view the brand or of somehow build brands into different categories. Some of them are broad and some are narrow single pool and Netflix streaming markets or Pepsi versus Coke and carbonated beverages market. In this case a frame of reference is narrow because there are only a few players in the field. So compare them with each other or both car market. This context is a lot more complicated since there are lots of car manufacturers. I think its difficult to compare them both explain to only a few new firms manage to compete in that market. It is just too hard to communicate your brand. Well there are already many other brands. After looking at the converging frame of reference we should think how to properly create in customers mind there are points of difference to customers trying to associate with specific brand. Let's look at some examples. DHL is often associated with fast and reliable delivery or his associates. Was lots of fun joy and entertainment. There are also so-called points of parity that *are benefits that are not unique but they are shared with other brands. There are two types of points of parity category as compared category points of piracy. Are those features that customers find essential. For example ofo the cameras are expected to cost good quality video as well. Combatted points of parity are used to overcome weaknesses of the brand. For instance Maybe dongs lost a lot of customers because they big healthy lifestyle became a major concern for a lot of people and obviously don't even associate with a healthy lifestyle. So consumers so to prefer other chains over the McDonalds to overcome that problem created more products that are related to a healthier life such as salads and smoothies. Their intent was not to make McDonalds appear as a healthy eating destination but reduce the weakness of the brand and retain customers. I hope that example was clear enough in this case. Healthy products are a comparative point of parity in McDonalds a branch positioned in such a way that it has both points of parity and points of difference if a brand has no points of parity. Customers have nothing to compare it to. Therefore customers will be uncertain about the product. On the other hand if there are no points of difference then there is no reason why with customer buy the product whatsoever. I should also mention that there are other more traditional approaches to positioning namely cultural branding and brand storytelling. Cultural branding as the name suggests is positioning the brand as a cultural phenomenon. Other* words should be connected to history and reflects culture. Let's talk about Ikea. It was followed in Sweden during the Second World War and is best known for a successful interplay of low cost and good quality. It reflects Swedish culture quite well. Swedish people spend their money carefully and live humbly brand story telling stories are widely used and brenne to create a of connection with an audience. Examples of companies that use storytelling in the right way are Nike and Go Pro. Go Pro constantly upload videos of different experiences of their users. They want to emphasize the Go Pro is more than just an action camera but a lifestyle filled with traveling adventures and new experiences. Let's consider Nike. Recently there is a campaign aimed at promoting fairness and diversity through the power of sport. Again that Nike Huyler's the idea behind the product rather than the product itself. All right guys. Super Tuesday.

PR activities

We're going to talk about public relations or more commonly PR public relations activities are the way firms or individuals create a positive image of what they're doing and create a tight relationship with their audiences. Some notable examples of successful PR campaigns include Google fights against Ebola. Some are sharing. Share a coke with an I Love New York campaign. There are numerous ways how we can inform the public and boost your reputation. You can find a journalist who is interested in writing about your life and career. You can organize events and experiences and to promote your or your firm's image. You can give interviews you can openly support ideas of other organizations such as charity organizations think of ICE BUCKET CHALLENGE you support charity and increase your visibility. That's a win scenario. Possibilities are endless. And the question of the day is isn't advertising and we heard the same thing. No. Knows why advertising is what we pay for publicity is only pray for advertising those with exposure while PR builds long term trust. What I would suggest is be careful. Mass media never sleeps and once you got in the game you're not leaving it at an action that you make now can wait for your reputation.

Section 7: Marketing budget

Marketing budget

you've come to the end of this book will learn quite a lot about deeper marketing activities and goes without saying that they need a solid budget in this very short book or shows some way set up a proper marketing budget statement percentage of revenue modeled in this method should a specific percentage of your revenues to cover up your marketing expenses. In most cases it ranges from 1 to 10 percent. This method is progressive in the sense that marketing costs are linked with revenues and therefore can change depending on the current situation. Second this model is the lack of flexibility. If your revenue doubles you may want to raise the bar. Same goes for the opposite scenario. If consumers are no longer buying the product it might be wise to redirect your budget for marketing to something else. Gold the Rohtak method . This one is straightforward. You allocate an optimal amount of money to achieve a specific outcome. So you want 10 percent market share in your field or increase profitability by 20 percent this year. You direct marketing costs to attain this specific goal although this murderous focus is static. Your goal may be want to. While there are costs that may change just in the shorter the gunmaker consider adjusting your budget accordingly. If parity mattered in this one you look at competitors and cyclospora them in terms of expenses. For example if Dave and Nick from our neighborhood spend 600 bucks on Facebook ads and they are doing fine then you should do quite the same. Honestly I do not recommend this method since you have no proof that competition achieves is a ghost in the most efficient way. Sometimes you could do *more and spend less. This method might only be suitable as a starting point but is not effective in general budget history that you compare your performance in two different time periods. If you achieve the desired outcome then there is no need to change the budget. There are problems then budget should be reconsidered. This matter may come handy soon is strongly tied up with your personal situation. On the other hand marketing is unpredictable and dynamic. Assuming if last year it worked then it should work. Hope this book gives you some ideas on how you can approach your budgeting. Thank you so much for reading.*

Section 8: Bonus lecture & Last words

Ethical Issues in Marketing

Did you know that 92 percent of millennials are more likely to buy products from firms who behave ethically in this page. We're going to talk about ethical and socially responsible marketing as being noise. And one of the first lectures effects of marketing can extend beyond the boundaries of noble ization and apply to the whole society. Therefore marketing managers must consider the ethical and environmental factors that are tied to their business. That's all marketing means showing the benefits of your product not just the customers but showing how the benefit to community and world around us will start by explaining what it means to be an article or. We're going to examine specific examples of unacceptable marketing practices. There are certain characteristics that define tactical and social responsible marketing which are safety. Make sure your product does no harm to the user or the environment otherwise should have clear advisory and Warnecke honesty. Ensure that your product satisfies what you promised to not deceive customers or anyone in the long run. Don't be a sword and dust your business. Transparency not fact or manipulate people Lord to stimulate a purchase. Being unethical in that regard is also illegal. I spoke to a customer and his privacy. If someone is willing to give some of his privacy information such as date of birth number of credit card or personal issues are not allowed to share it to third parties because all the customers permission. The whole intrusion to the truth is that the third party is the government respects your competitors. Never bad mouth organizations or individuals that compete because you don't know what marketing is all *about. Let's talk about the most prominent and single issues related to marketing misleading claims. The 1950s in the US tobacco used to be advertised as promo's because negative advertising highlighting compacter products is downsized rather than showing the adventures of your own product. That's what Sun and Apple are doing. Post-purchase dishonors the company and told that you will get. Doesn't match what you've got. You've probably experienced that food looks much better on the images than reality. Spam fill in customers voice mail email or social media with our requested messages green washing. Just putting the label to it that you care about the environment while in reality you are not targeting the vulnerable groups. For example in Belgium it is banned to show commercials during children's programs.*

Last words for this book

You are officially finished this book. I just want to say thank you for your time and attention. That means the world to me. I hope you had a good time reading this book because I had a great time teaching you. I can only ask one thing from you if you enjoyed the book. Please spread the words and leave a positive review that will help me a lot. It goes without saying if you want a Learn more or suggest something. Be sure to Destini or both questions in discussion forum at any time. That being said I hope you will use the knowledge gained from the book and I wish you success by everyone.

www.ingramcontent.com/pod-product-compliance
Lightning Source LLC
Chambersburg PA
CBHW050309220526
45465CB00005B/1922